Life's Licks with the Help of My Sage Turtle's Horn

Jill Victoria Bicoy DeHayward

VANTAGE PRESS
New York

Cover design by Polly McQuillen

FIRST EDITION

Copyright © 2006 by Jill Victoria Bicoy DeHayward

Published by Vantage Press, Inc.
419 Park Ave. South, New York, NY 10016

Manufactured in the United States of America
ISBN: 0-533-14373-X

Library of Congress Catalog Card No.: 2002092972

0 9 8 7 6 5 4 3 2 1

This part of my work is dedicated to my father. Without his sage wisdom, this book would never have been written. He taught me that if you want to get your point across to people, use the simplest language that you can; so I have created the enclosed poems and/or song lyrics to be just as simple as possible, but to leave the reader with messages or food for thought like a "light bulb" has gone on in his/her head.

I want readers to come away from them smiling, hopeful, thinking positively, with insight food for thought, closer to HIS image, and also come away having taken and shared a part of me. . . .

I call these poems and song lyrics "LIFE'S LICKS IN POETIC QUIPS WITH THE HELP OF MY SAGE TURTLE'S HORN."

Contents

Life's Licks in Poetic Quips
with the Help of My Sage Turtle's Horn

Walking, Just Walking in the Rain

I couldn't feel the difference,
between the rain drops and my tears,
while wiping away the wet drops,
thought of memories of many years.

Why did you deceive me?
Did you think I wouldn't know?
Why were you unfaithful,
when I loved you so . . .

Was it my imagination,
when I felt I was yours and you were mine?
When did you stop feeling this way?
Why did you make me feel everything's fine?

When you are having an affair,
and you think no one will ever know,
but because of many years together,
the sudden changes to me will show.

So here I am, walking in the rain,
hoping the tears and rain drops will help keep me sane;
so here I am, walking in the rain;
walking to stop the hurt, walking to stop the pain. . . .

So here I am, just walking in the rain;
just walking . . . just walking in the rain . . .

What a Difference Does Love Make

What a difference does love make;
all the years, days and hours;
what a difference does love make;
through seasons and spring showers;

What a difference does love make;
the difference is you. . . .

What a difference does love make,
during sleeping and dawn hours;
what a difference does love make,
making love between lovers;

What a difference does love make;
the difference is you. . . .

When seeing your face and smile,
and admiring your provocative style,
makes me want you in my life forever,
never, never to part, not ever;

What a difference does love make;
the difference is you.

Yes, the difference is you. . . .

(This may sound repetitious, but it can be used as lyrics for a
song.)

I'll Be There

If there's a heaven I will be there;
because I know that's where you'll be.
When you leave here, you'll go there;
and you'll be waiting for me.

Straight up to heaven I'll go,
to earn my angel's wings;
straight up to where I know,
the white love dove sings.

So wait for me, my darling;
I'll be there and real soon,
passing all the bright stars,
even passing the moon.

If there's a heaven I'll be there;
just you wait and see;
because I know you'll be there, too,
waiting there for me.

If there's a heaven I'll be there;
yes, I'll be there. . . .

I'll be there. . . .

Blues on Parade

Blues on parade;
the heat's on and there's no shade;
blues on parade . . .

Blues on parade;
close to a Royal Flush, but where's that spade?
Blues on parade . . .

Blues on parade;
had a job, company's closed, thought I had it made;
blues on parade . . .

Blues on parade;
lost my good wife; now have a lazy maid;
blues on parade . . .

Give me an even break;
there's not much more I can take;
get me off this merry-go-round;
head straight but feet on the ground. . . .

Blues on parade
Blues on parade
Blues on parade.

(This could be used as jazz lyrics. I didn't want to make it too
depressing . . . we have enough of that in this world.)

If You Could See

If you could see like me,
could be you'd see
the recesses of my mind.
If you could see like me,
could be you'd see;
thought processes of a special kind.
This conversation will be
independent of the usual kind;
and could be you'll see,
how to love (so simple); it'll blow your mind.
If you could see like me,
could be you'd see,
it's easier a lover be.
If you could see like me,
could be you'd see;
how easy loving can be.
If you could see like me,
could be you'd see,
a simple lesson to learn.

MAKE YOURSELF EASIER TO LOVE;
AND YOU'LL FIND LOVE AND BE LOVED IN
    RETURN . . .

If you could see . . .
If you could see. . . .

(This poem was written as a simple repetitive play on
words; but it still leaves a message for thought.)

When We Kiss in the Moonlight

When we kiss in the moonlight,
it is so very clear;
that in each other's arms;
where we feel most secure.

When we kiss in the moonlight,
the nights seem too short and days too long;
our thoughts are always of each other;
in each other's arms we want to belong.

Even if the time's short when we we're together;
the quality of time always gave us much pleasure.
Even when we did or thought something wrong,
of each other, our love always remained strong.

When we kiss in the moonlight,
our hearts beat as one.
When we kiss in the moonlight,
the moon shone like the sun.

When we kiss in the moonlight,
starry eyed—this is where we want to stay.
Kissing in the moonlight
kissing in the moonlight

When we kiss in the moonlight. . . .

Sage Turtle, Come Blow Your Horn

When I was but a little girl,
never thought my papa would go away;
and when the Angels came to take him,
it was such a sad, sad day. . . .
I was older than when Papa died;
I remember grieving so oh, how I cried;
though many years have gone by;
on Father's Day I still for Papa would cry.
Sometimes I find myself talking to him;
though I know no longer is he here;
but I believe wherever he is in heaven,
he's never too busy to hear me up there.
Anyway, I keep remembering his words before he went
    away;
that cold, misty and very sad gray day.
"When live physically hindered was he to places go or
    loved ones to see;
but in death, unhindered is he to places go or with loved
    ones be."
My Sage Turtle to me this did mention,
so I know he visits me whenever he comes down from
    heaven;
I know he'll always my Sage Turtle HERO be;
because of all Sage wisdom he shared, and all the love he
    gave me. . . .
But still I wish with the Angels he did not go;
because I miss my Papa still; I miss my Sage Turtle so. . . .
I miss my SAGE TURTLE so. . . .

From the Bottom of the Barrel

From the bottom of the barrel
next step would be to go barrel's way up;
but turn the barrel upside down;
and you'll find the bottom's no different from the top.

This is my poetic quips way to say;
I appreciate all that I have today;
for this is where many may wish to be;
especially those who are less fortunate than me.

And the times I tried taking barrel's straight way up;
this was not to my benefit and wise I found;
for though I was no longer on barrel's bottom ground;
at top I found—the direction I was headed
was still facing down . . .

Yep, like that barrel, no short cuts
in life one should take,
and the quick fixes aren't wise
and one should never make . . .

Like that barrel, life's easier and more rewarding I found;
not to take short cuts up, but barrel's long way round;
so when I get to the top, I'll still be looking up,
and the direction I'll be headed will no longer be down.

From the bottom of the barrel;
From the bottom of the barrel . . .

Turtle on Its Back

If you feel like a TURTLE on its back,
with no one to put you on your fours again,
like the TURTLE, be glad he still had
his firm hard shell to lie in . . .

No matter what the situation
or how depressing and dismal it could be too,
there's always many, many others
who are far less fortunate than you . . .

And it's always wise to keep a "sense of humor" intact;
many times "sense of humor" will help bring sense of
     balance back;
this is another of my poetic quips way to say that I'm
     A.O.K.
of what I have and who I am today . . .

And whenever there's wants and I forget,
I think of that TURTLE on his back;
keeps me humble, my spirits up;
and all my mental faculties intact . . .

Like the TURTLE on his back;
like the TURTLE on his back . . .

Ache in My Heart

There's an ache in my heart so deep;
and no ending to the tears when I weep;
like depth of the ocean never running dry;
no ending to the tears when I cry . . .
There's an ache that tries to invade;
the deepest recessions of my heart,
where I don't allow many people in;
when I do, keep inside me; never to part.
Why do I feel this way? So sad so forlorn;
feeling a great wave of sadness coming on;
as if I sense there's something that's coming my way,
that will explain the reason I'm feeling like this today.
Afraid to answer the phone or open the door;
to me, this has never happened before,
as if I know there's something wrong;
and a great sadness for me was in store.
Then it came, the answer; the very sad news;
so difficult to accept; I angrily refuse;
a **DRUNK DRIVER** killed part of my family;
young and so vital they were: a baby and ages twenty-two
    & twenty-three:
it was quick they say; felt they no pain;
but this ache in me continues just the same . . .
Now I understand why; and don't question the MAN;
and trying I am to keep in control the best I can;
but there's still a deep ache in my heart,
a deep ache in my heart . . .
a deep ache in my heart . . .

This Is a Woman

This is a WOMAN who feels with her heart,
even when hers is breaking apart.

This is a WOMAN who thinks with her heart;
while those thinking they're clever; really are not.

This is a WOMAN who loves with her heart,
because loving well, is part of her art.

This is a WOMAN who sees with her heart,
she sees, what those who can see, will not.

This is a WOMAN who prays with her heart,
because she knows; from him, she had life's start.

This is a WOMAN who cries with her heart,
because tenderness and her heart are never apart.

This is a WOMAN who hears with her heart;
she hears, what those who can hear; will not.

This is a WOMAN "GOD" LOVES WITH HIS HEART;
HIS and her IMAGES are one and never apart.

This is a WOMAN, yes, this is a WOMAN
who LIVES with her HEART;
Yes, this is a WOMAN who lives with her heart;
THIS IS A WOMAN.

(This poem was created in honor of MS. ELIZABETH
TAYLOR. I think she's a beautiful person with a "settled
soul.")

The Unborn Child
(Abortion question)

Lovers' intimate indiscretions
should never end with a choice so vile;
as to condone taking the life
of an innocent unborn child. . . .
For hand none the child had
in its own impregnation,
so why should the child
be denied (his/her) own creation?

Mothers-to-be, don't make lovers' mistake;
it's murder in all eyes for a life to take;
a life is a life and should not
be mother's choice that it be taken;
it's the LORD'S choice to allow
these beautiful souls to come down
or to stay in heaven.

It's HE who giveth or taketh life away,
or whether we cease to exist tomorrow or today;
a child's life should never be taken;
because of a parent's sexual mistake;
life instead, should be given;
and other parents will happier make.

It's common sense too
for politicians not to do;
that's to act like political fools;
to help make immoral laws;
that contradict GOD'S RULES. . . .

So take careful heed
and beware all the while,
who loses really . . .
When we take the life
of an unborn child.

The life of an unborn child.

I Remember When

I remember when I was a little girl;
when Papa and I were playing on the green grass;
the day was fun and so beautiful;
I wanted the special day to last.

Birds came flying above the blue sky;
they were so beautiful—spreading their wings up high.
Where are they going? Where did they come from?
"Papa," I asked, "and why?"

"Just enjoy what you now see about the birds
as they fly across the blue Hawaii sky;
Someday, Angel, you'll go away;
and you'll find all the answers and why.

"And when you do, you'll come home too;
and play on the same green grass;
and see the same lofty blue sky,

"Then you'll see birds flying across the sky;
won't ask your papa the answers you seeked;
because you already know why."

Strangest thing happened and Papa answered why;
I didn't enjoy the birds as much this time,
as they flew on by. . . .

Papa says, "This happens all the time;
it comes from growing up too soon,
learning too much and too fast,

"Enjoy the beautiful things
that give you pleasure as a child;
don't question it and the beauty
and wonderment for you will last.

"Growing up too fast and too soon—one loses those
        special ties,
of this beautiful world that's seen only through a child's
        eyes."

I remember when my papa shared this wisdom with me;
since, I never for the answers about how the birds looked
        to see;
I will never want to break those childlike ties;
Because I enjoy the wonderment when looking at this
        world
through childlike eyes. . . .

Record on a Shelf

One can, like a record can life,
and place it on a dusty and lonely shelf;
and what a fool one can be,
if an illness had he, and added making
an invalid of himself. . . .

If life's record had I been given,
and had I placed on a dismal shelf,
and for myself kept life from spinning,
then no bigger fool have I encountered,
than one made I of myself. . . .

So took the time to look further than I am; further than
    myself;
lifted I the dusty lid, and got off the burdened shelf;
so got off the shelf I did and flipped onto the lighter side
    of life;
I've found living life much easier; even in lonely times of
    strife.

And more tragic would it be for me,
if even before my life's record was played,
if so spun around with defeat was I;
and on the lonely shelf stayed. . . .

And besides making a handicap of hang-up,
had already a "dead beat" made of myself;
so come on, girl; get off, get off that shelf!

GET OFF THAT SHELF.

Success

When Life's success seems stagnant
and wished more in our lives had we,
I always thought of the wise words
my Father had once taught me. . . .

"Even if gained a man all the wealth in the world"
less fortunate would he still be,
to a man who found the worth of his soul;
and the formula for "SUCCESSFUL LIVING" had he.

"MONEY," he said, "should never be used"
as a slide rule with which "TRUE SUCCESS" be measured;
or "GENUINE HAPPINESS" be met.
For life's many successes are measured instead,
by the degree of "HAPPINESS" that one out of life hopes
     to get;

That feeling of "CONTENTED ENJOYMENT"
one hopes to derive out of whatever in life he does;
Now . . . when I stop to think of "SUCCESS,"
I THINK OF "HAPPINESS"
AND HOW WISE MY FATHER WAS. . . .

How Goes Our Country?

How goes our country?
Ask we this question?
Wars, riots, lootings,
marches, burnings, shootings;
surely an answer there must be.
Ask we this question:
how goes our country?

Concerned we are not of problems far;
leave it to leaders and officials;
but when tragedy hits where we are,
fault it is always of others.

When all goes not well, good it is to remember this of our
     country;
ruled by a few we are not; but by a "PRINCIPLE" called
     "DEMOCRACY";
it is choice "OURS" or votes our leaders be, president and
     others;
but remember, for it's important; it is "WE THE PEOPLE
     WHO ARE THE LEADERS."

It is not the elected officials
who citizens' actions of laws decide;
but system and office heads only;
it is "WE," our wishes they are to guide,
if this COUNTRY BE A "DEMOCRACY."

To See; But Not to See

It is all so senseless our conflicts of skin;
have we not enough our neurosis within?
"Common Sense" 'tis all the answer be;
for those not blind, but cannot see. . . .

Who is to judge
better color of skin?
When in death,
flesh falls,
all bones white,
all when live,
blood red within. . . .

If search we of late
our conscience bare
the answer is such
as it always been;
judge we never;
not of others,
their respect,
their rights,
by the color of their skin. . . .

Respect, importance, rights,
we have not to ourselves give
or from others this expect,
if in your hearts kindles this "PREJUDICE"
and did not correct.

"Can't Get Myself Together"
(Can't be me)

Ever since you've been gone,
the days have been much too long;
I can't seem to get myself together;
find myself always wearing your sweater.

Can't let go of your many years with me;
it's been so many happy, happy years, you see;
nothing's important anymore, nothing matters;
I just can't seem to get myself together.

Why, oh why, did you go away and leave me here alone to
        stay;
and when the Angels came they should have taken us both
        away;
and now it's too late for the many things I wanted still to
        say;
how much I loved you, wanted you; how proud I was of
        you every day.

Here I am, wrapped close around me your sweater,
taking in the fragrance of cologne we picked together;
I sit and weep; never been a "Down Beat," but, dear, can't
        you see?
The many years together, became one, so without you I
        can't be me. . . .

I don't think I want to stay alone
here in this dimension any longer;
want to be where you are;
so we could be together. . . .

I just can't be me any longer;
I just can't get myself together. . . .

Be Still My Heart

I loved you, Dear Heart, more so now then ever;
and this I would like for you to remember,
though you may have hurt and caused me pain;
to question my love you need not, ever again. . . .

Though I will miss you and want you, my love;
and will hurt for a very long, long time;
I do forgive you and judge you not;
for she's loved you well, this heart of mine.

But for now, I wish my heart's giving will to me be as
    kind,
freeing this longing and setting free this deep hurt of mine;
then too, I can honestly say, though no longer will we be
    together;
my heart and I had gone away with a love that will go on
    forever.

The pain be now as such, that what I ask, does not seem
    much;
how I wish I could of it ask and compassionately my heart
    will,
heart of mine; hold fast this love and be kind,
weep no more, beat no more, be still . . . be still . . .

We'd Like to Think

Hopes of Peace and Love,
      with genuine sense of "CARING"
and sincere attitude
      of unselfish giving
naturally shared
      with amongst us the "Living"
will into our lives
      bestow "Love"; "God's" beautiful meaning
more happiness and Faith too
      also be bringing
each and every year through
      as well as each "Christmas" season.

This is what "we'd like to think,"
      "Christmas" is all about
in our hearts kept always
      and never let out,
for "Peace" be futile
      even how hard we try
if in our hearts this feeling had
      but let die.

Not only of those close to us
      should we give time or bother,
try we should to live life too
      "caring" for our human brother,
whether in Vietnam
      or places much far;
"Caring" starts in our Hearts
      and just where we are.

One should show concern
       for his human brother,
starting to be friends
       with his next-door neighbor
and with you this feeling
       would also like to share
for "Peace" be difficult
       to survive or surface bare
if there not be more
       OF US WHO "CARE"

Grace under Fire

I, of myself
but once in my life
my "**Insight**" made blind
and found it most trying
and not at all easy;
to maintaining emotional
and mental composure;
be that of a woman
Who be a "**lady**".

The day I remember
so great was made
my emotional pressure;
because of "**Love's**" betrayal
my heart was painfully
made to suffer;

And it be that sad day
when felt I like
"**completely blowing my cool**"
and "**coming on strong**"
on a "**stage of rage**"
and with "**hysterics**"
be playing the "fool";

So hurt I **was**
the betrayal of love
there were no "**buts**"
about it or "**maybe**"
with tears from my eyes
blurred the vision of my heart
and in "**pain's**" way
in-line was she
so "**lost sight**"
the "**insight**" of me
could not see "**the lady**";

Coupled with keeping
emotions and faculties intact;
in "**broken heart's way**" was hard
to "**keep cool**" that day;
and impossible seem
to "**MAINTAIN GRACE UNDER FIRE**"
and not give way to "**BITTER REVENGE**"
an "**IMPUDENT**" desire;

YES, IT WAS ON THAT DAY
"LOST SIGHT" OF SHE
THE "INSIGHT" OF **ME**
"THE LADY" . . .

Gossip

I believe in your rights;
      freedom of speech is my delight.
But neighbors and friends;
      just so you'll know.
I refuse to hear "gossip"
      In my bungalow.
I find it contagious
      like the measles or the mumps.
I love to have company
      any time of the day,
But I'm warning you
      if you have come to stay,
Don't talk my friend down
      with gossip and dirt
Or you'll be finding yourself talking
      to the back of my shirt.
Smile, be gay—look at the good
      that is yet to be found
And it can, you know
      if you only look around.
I may lose a few friends
      but I won't mind you see.
My true friends will remain
      honest and true to me
For good or bad, what you do unto others
      will be done unto thee.

Santa Does His Thing

There are many of Santa's helpers
come Christmas time of year
who carried Santa's bag
with bills up to their ear.

And hard they find it not
for champagne to slowly sip,
for bigger the Santa's bag
the stiffer their upper lip.

Yet it gave them pleasure
though "small" their wallet size
to help fill Santa's treasure
for Christmas morning surprise.

It's Santa who gets the most credit
full stockings toys and all,
but it was Santa's helper
who really had a ball.

For daddies know and wise they be;
the years ahead they already see
will fly by fast then past will be
and what now is be a memory.

No longer stuffed stockings
by chimney hung with care
so full with goodies and little toys
each end up with a tear.

With great hopes that Santa
will the toy they wished for bring,
excited little children
carols would loudly sing.

Or with a straight firm face
would hear their daddy say,
"There's eight tiny reindeer
and a toy-filled sleigh;
and on Christmas Eve, hear you
jolly laughter or sleigh bells ring,
it's only good old Santa doing his thing.

And for Santa's helper
a tear I'll shed that day,
for a friend he's known so well
had sadly gone away.

And Christmas from then on
just be a wistful drag
for SANTA has and will always be
"A DADDY'S SPECIAL BAG!"

A Friend

A friend is someone
who comes into your heart
with all intentions to stay
and is always thought of
in a very special way.

By no false pretense had he
try to acquire this position
nor was the order of his friendship
ever judged or demand question.

Never afraid was he to make
our problems his personal affair;
never thought it as "buttin' in"
just simply because he did care.

A gentle hand, sympathetic composer
seemed always to be his style,
and in times of strife and trouble
would somehow make you smile.

He may not be around much
or the times many each other see,
but, when trouble did befall us
right by our sides he would be.

The things we do/did whether right or wrong
to him need not explain; or from need seek approval,
for a friend and that he was
did not need or cared for any
(which makes him even more special).

A friend is someone
who looks just to find
only that which is good in you
and with the same respect and due affection
you see him in the same light too . . .

THIS IS A FRIEND. . . .

(In this poem the female gender may be alternated by insert-
ing: She, her, etc.)

The Most Beautiful People in the World

They will always come to us
so preciously little in size
and will start even then
to affect many lives;
with one might come later.
A skateboard, doll, or bike;
and the taste of spinach too
most likely will not like;
they'll successfully manage too,
to get in grown-ups' way;
yet little is how we'd like
to always have them stay.

They are very beautiful,
each special little people,
and like a tree without a stem,
no home's complete without them.
All are shining stars really . . .
even when crying or acting silly;
and when on bended knee they pray;
a bit of heaven came down to stay.

With tears in our eyes
hard to someday realize
quickly the years had gone past,
our child had to let go at last;
I think our hearts knew this
when they into our arms first came,
though we try to understand
will hurt deeply all the same.

Question will we of ourselves,
"Has it been worth parents' while
to give life, love, and protect
only to let go of our child?"
Without doubt or question,
know we what the answer will be,
if had the years looked back
and happy memories did see.

And if we chose to be wise
and measured happiness not by size;
minute will seem their monetary cost
for gained more had we and nothing lost;
"HAPPINESS" can also be described and felt
to be genuine and true;
if in your arms have come and held you
one of these BEAUTIFUL PEOPLE too.

Who may they be?
Of those I am talking about?
They who could grow
tall, short, skinny or stout?
Who softly could speak
but mostly like to shout;
who also slowly could walk;
but mostly ran about?
Who may they be?
Who, when "LITTLE" be most
PRECIOUS to see?

It's CHILDREN, CHILDREN,
CHILDREN;
It's CHILDREN they be;
who from LOVERS' arms unfurled;
and into ours as PARENTS have come;
"CHILDREN," "THE MOST BEAUTIFUL
PEOPLE IN THE WORLD."

How do I know? BECAUSE I HAVE SOME!

It's Easier Said than Done

I remember as a little girl
a very wise story I once read
the years past for forgetting;
I remembered it instead,
because of the humor I saw,
and how much like "mice" people can be
and the philosophy of which
inwardly was meant for us to see.

Frightened were a bunch of little house mice
of a big, big cat more mean than nice.
The mice decided to take care of the matter,
putting their ideas and heads together;
"We'd tie a bell round the cat's neck;
we'd hear the bell at his each step;
we can hide ourselves in plenty of time;
with the ringing as our warning sign!"

But to tie the bell around the cat's neck;
whose thought to do that?!

Too, like those mice we can
try to solve a problem,
and come up with what
may seem like a wonderful plan;
but also like those mice,
never ask ourselves beforehand;
"Can we carry it out?"
And will the answer be;
"Yes, we can!"

Though there be many times
we'll find it easy for plans
in our minds to come about;
but, we'll also find
how much easier it is
to think up a plan
"than to carry it out!"

A Very Big, Big Fly

A fly was buzzing around the house,
by the end of day gotten tired
and looked for a place to rest instead
upon which he bounced and buzzed
giving testimonial to his weight;
the place he found;
the top of our Bassett's head.

The fly seemed persistent that his presence be known;
as if his weight should be felt, thus his status shown;
"Sir," said the fly, "Please pardon the sudden weight
and intrusion. I'll just rest a while then fly away,
ridding you of this heavy burden."

But of his weight, ne'r stirred our Bassett, or flapped
he an ear; said instead, "Oh! Little fly, didn't know you
were here! Do as you like, didn't feel you when you first
came, and after you've left, I'll still feel the same."

Sometimes the biggest people
can foolishly make themselves
look like little elves;
and sometimes, the smallest people
have the biggest opinions of themselves.

Come Fly with Me

Come fly with me
come fly away
and see the world
that we can unfurl
in another way.

Come fly with me
come fly away
and you will see
a lovelier place this world could be;
upon which to stay.

Though I know it's been disappointing
daily news and world in its review,
but there's another kind of world
that holds beauty and wonderment too.

Come fly with me
come fly away
and I'll show you how
to get away
and see a better world somehow.

Come fly with me
come fly away
and I'll share with you my wonderment ties
for a better vision of the world
through "CHILD-LIKE EYES"
Come fly with me . . .
come fly with me. . . .
Come fly away. . . .

What Is a Home?

A HOME IS NOT A PLACE
just where your wife and children are;

A HOME IS NOT A PLACE
where you park your special car;

A HOME IS NOT A PLACE
where your prize possessions are kept;

A HOME IS NOT A PLACE
where your sexual needs are met;

A HOME IS NOT A PLACE
where all your meals go to eat;

A HOME IS NOT A PLACE
where all your old friends meet;

A HOME IS A HOME
where your "HEART" is, and loved ones in you believe;

A HOME IS A PLACE
where you want to go to; and never want to leave. . . .

Maybe Someday

Though you left us and took your wants with you,
you left behind with your family your love and heart too;
I feel this deeply and without the slightest doubt;
that you will want us again when you know what's your
    life is about.

We forgive and do not judge you and happy we wish you
    to be;
those who love you very much; your children and me;
MAYBE SOMEDAY, you'll want us in your life and want
    us back again;
but, darling, for now it's good-bye; and maybe, just
    maybe;
we'll be together again.

So be happy, dear heart, wherever you may be or go;
we'll be wanting it very much for you to be so;
maybe someday you'll find yourself wanting and looking
    for us too;
and we hope then, that we'll still be wanting to be with
    you.

But, darling, when the time comes, if it does; you'll find us
    not very far;
Never further than heart's way, never further than where
    you are;
for every day, as sure as the sun rises and as it will set,
the love and memory of us will haunt you,
though you may try; but you will never forget.

I Have a Good Heart

I have a good heart;
it always has been kind;
and with "loving" intertwined;
and in "giving" wouldn't part;
"I HAVE A GOOD HEART."

I have a good heart;
the pains of past always let go;
and sorrows of tomorrow will not show;
"I HAVE A GOOD HEART."

Though there were times she could remember,
when "love" to her had been unkind;
but then she's so "forgiving" and "tender,"
she "loves well" this heart of mine.

I have a good heart;
she makes life easier I found;
living life day by day;
and "loving" all year round;
"I HAVE A GOOD HEART"
"I HAVE A GOOD HEART."

Yes, I do HAVE A GOOD HEART. . . .

Shoot for the Moon

"GO FOR PERFECTION"
whenever you can;
don't settle for just "good" or "better";
if more of yourself you can demand!

"GO FOR PERFECTION"
in whatever you do
and the finished product,
you'll like better too.

You'll be wonderfully amazed
at what you will find;
and how "GREAT" your "BEST"
will be when leaving "Good" or "Better" behind;

"SHOOTING FOR PERFECTION"
a happier person will be;
of the finished "product"
or "relationships" others to see;

Anyway, what could happen really?
If you did "SHOOT FOR THE MOON";
maybe, even Venus or Mars;
and if missed and your "BEST"
WAS LANDING ON THE STARS!

LANDING ON THE STARS . . .

Hey There

HEY THERE,
you with your head in the clouds,
has love made you so blind;
that you've wiped insight;
out of your mind.

HEY THERE,
can't you see he's not just for you?
'Cause he's making plays for others too?
"You're the only one," he said, "and I love you";
But he's said the same thing to others too.

HEY THERE,
don't be a love-sick fool
and come down out of the clouds;
take yourself out of his pool;

Of other women like yourself
and whose just as blind;
and whose affection he also toyed with;
with only one thing in mind.

HEY THERE,
don't go on as if you're blind
and give him what he has in mind;
soon enough he'll play himself out
and then you'll know what he's all about.

HEY THERE . . .
HEY THERE. . . .

State of Mind

When I look around
at this changing world,
I can't imagine how it would be
without this special place
I've created for me.

This place I love so much,
and only those I love will allow to touch;
this place in others I can believe;
this place where I can go;
and not want to leave . . .

Where can you find a special place like this
that one searches a lifetime for and doesn't want to miss;
this special place is never very far;
look for the "SILVER LINING" and you'll find it's where
     you are.

This place in "receiving,"
in "giving" will be easy to find;
this place is a special place;
it's a "STATE OF MIND";
a "STATE OF MIND" . . .

Don't Bother about Me

DON'T BOTHER ABOUT ME,
I'll be around;
DON'T BOTHER ABOUT ME,
I'll be strong;
DON'T BOTHER ABOUT ME,
I'll find ways; to fill my days;
DON'T BOTHER ABOUT ME. . . .

DON'T BOTHER ABOUT ME,
My feet are on the ground;
DON'T BOTHER ABOUT ME,
to loneliness I won't be bound;
this about me; you will see;
DON'T BOTHER ABOUT ME. . . .

There's always a way to cope with a broken heart;
and it's been so long since we've been apart;
so I can't start with tears in my heart;
to give "living" again a good start.

DON'T BOTHER ABOUT ME,
I'll be just OK.
I'll take my new life,
living day by day;
so DON'T BOTHER ABOUT ME,
DON'T BOTHER ABOUT ME.

Strings to My Heart

There's not a day that goes by
that a tear doesn't shed from my eyes,
of days when I remember,
that mid-November to September;

When so in pain were you
and there wasn't a thing I could do;
but hold your hand and pray;
for the suffering to go away.

Then came that day late in September,
when the Angels came and took you away;
glad I was of that final sleep of peace;
that God had given you that day. . . .

Though no longer will you suffer,
and glad was I of this;
but, darling, I miss our life together,
and most of all; it's you I miss;
darling, it's you I really miss. . . .

Though you're now up in "heaven" to stay,
I still miss you in every way;
and though you and I are now apart,
YOU STILL HOLD THE STRINGS TO MY HEART.
THE STRINGS TO MY HEART. . . .

I Will Remember You

I will remember you
in the "flowers" of Spring and the "warmth" of Summer!
I will remember you
in the "bright colors" of Autumn and the "cool" of Winter;
I will remember you.

I will remember you
loving all the seasons of the year;
I will remember you
because I still love you dear;
I will remember you.

No words could ever explain how wonderful it was loving
    you;
and better still it was, when you really loved me too;
knowing you'd hurt me; never told me you were fatally ill;
and now you're gone, dear; but my heart loves you still.

I'll remember you in dawn of each morn,
and sunset of each day too;
and when I hear the lilt of laughter,
I will remember you; I will remember you. . . .

I will remember you. . . .

Star Dust in Her Hair

When she walked into the room,
she lightened up my heart;
like the candles on the chandelier,
couldn't tell them apart;

A glowing "aura" that she had,
like "star dust" was in her hair;
so beautiful she was;
of others I wasn't aware;

When she smiled she lit a thousand candles in my heart;
she lightened my heart and my head went reeling;
between my head and my heart, they both kept spinning;
I was "star struck" with the Angel with "star dust."

If she had asked I'd follow
her to the moon; anywhere;
this Angel with "Star Dust"
in her hair;

How she's lightened my life
this Angel of giving;
she's now given me
a good reason for living.

This Angel of mine with the "star dust"
in her hair . . .

Melody in My Heart

There's a melody in my heart
everytime you come near;
my heart plays like a harp;
"Haunting" the melody I hear;

There's a melody in my heart
that lightens now my days,
with melodic notes of "love,"
"touching" cells of my being in special ways;

Though when alone, I feel very content;
with this melody that feels God-sent,
I feel "happiness" in whatever I do;
with "love's" melody and the "existence" of you.

There's a melody in my heart;
I'm sure to many this isn't new;
but it makes me feel so "alive"
to want you and love you too.

There's a melody in my heart;
There's a melody in my heart. . . .

Sometimes It's True

SOMETIMES IT'S TRUE;
There are those
who walk this world with "blinders" on;
have eyes to see;
but can't see what's wrong;

SOMETIMES IT'S TRUE;
they see the world
through purple-colored glasses;
never seeing life for real;
or if they've really lived until life passes;

Yet sometimes this may not seem so very wrong,
for those who say they are; but really are not strong;
to live their lives with "blinders" or "purple glasses" on,
shielding themselves from undue stress and pain; till from
    this
earth gone.

SOMETIMES IT'S TRUE;
there's many who live life this way,
and though many think it wrong;
this is how they live day by day
and are very happy their whole life long;

And whether it's right or wrong;
it's their lives they're living (not ours) all along.

If You Live in Glass Houses
(Don't throw stones)

We had next-door neighbors,
who would always (loudly) fight;
as if this gave them great delight;
they also had a big dog that barked a lot
and was taught also to bite;

The other neighbors kept moving,
one family after the other;
they couldn't take them anymore,
and didn't want their bother;

Then one day, two men passed by
and started arguing; annoyed was our dog;
so he started barking;
The neighbor came out and yelled to stop the "darn"
    noise;
I found it difficult to maintain my poise;

Our neighbors came out
and hit our dog with stones;
I took the dog to the Vet
and was told he had two broken bones;

Angry I was and felt they could not atone,
for the dog's two broken bones;
and "those who live in glass houses should never thrown
    stones!
"SHOULD NEVER THROW STONES!"

Roller Coaster Ride

Life can be like a "roller coaster" ride,
the "ups" and "downs,"
the real "highs" and real "lows,"
sometimes right actions **hard to decide;**

Though how hard we try,
just don't know why—get out of coaster track,
and get stymied at coaster's dips and turns;
and though how hard we tried, it wasn't easy
to get back;

But though we get discouraged,
give yourselves "A" for "Effort" and "Tenacity";
for it's not the "trying" that really gets us down;
but the "procrastinations" and lack of "veracity";

Life's "roller coaster" ride can really be fun
if from it you can see life's "silver lining";
for it's really how we handle the "downs" that make
the "ups" worthwhile; giving greater meaning and value
to "living."

So life's "roller coaster" ride can be challenging,
not boring and a lot of fun;
but this, one will never know
unless one had "the courage" to try one.

If I Had a Crystal Ball

IF I HAD A CRYSTAL BALL,
I'd foresee all sorts things;
a home for my daughter,
a car for my brother,
and for Mama a diamond ring;

IF I HAD A CRYSTAL BALL,
I'd foresee much LOVE for all;
love between races,
love among countries,
love for each other ALL;

There are so many things;
if only to foresee; would bring;
and most important of all,
I'd foresee much happiness for all;

IF I HAD A CRYSTAL BALL,
In the future there would only be;
peace between races
peace among countries
peace for you and me;

IF I HAD A CRYSTAL BALL,
I'd foresee the "best" for all;
if I had a crystal ball,
if I had a crystal ball. . . .

The "Hula" Omi, Omi
(Pronunciation O-MEE)

Swing it left and swing it right
OMI, OMI left; OMI, OMI right;
and OMI, OMI all around;
to HAWAIIAN rhythm and sound;

With "HULA" hands, fun it is;
telling story, with vamping feet;
OMI to the left, OMI to the right;
OMI all around to OMI, OMI beat;

One can't do the "HULA"
without learning how to "OMI";
I saw it once and liked it,
so I asked the dancer to show me;

Now I can OMI to the left;
and OMI to the right;
and OMI, OMI all around;
I can OMI all night;

TO "HAWAIIAN" HULA
DANCE AND MUSICAL SOUND. . . .

I Wanna Go Back to My Island Shack

I wanna go back
to my island shack;
near KAU-NA-KA-KAI
on MO-LO-KAI;

Where the trade winds blow
and whisper by the clear blue sea;
and the white sandy beaches
keep beckoning and "haunting" me;

Come to my warm white sands and on them lie;
Come see the Kanis and Wahinees in bikinis stroll by;
Come to where your loving family are the real stars;
Come to where there's no "grid" and so many cars;

I wanna go back
to my island shack;
near KAU-NA-KA-KAI;
on MO-LO-KAI;

To MO-LO-KAI
a tropical isle by the sea,
one of the beautiful islands;
in the STATE OF HA-VA-II;
STATE OF HA-VA-II.

(I was born on the island of Molokai, Hawaii; and yes, not
far from the town of Kaunakakai, and the proper pronuncia-
tion of HAWAII is HA-VA-II. The 'W' is supposed to sound
like a 'V.' Pronounce Kaunakakai and Molokai phonetically
as is written and you'll be saying it right.)

I Looked to the Wind to Dry My Tears

The wind was cold and blowing;
the leaves were scattering and branches swaying;
and my heart had been broken and there were fears;
so I couldn't see the trees through my tears;

I walked in the cold and windy mist;
with the wind blowing through my hair;
Love's betrayal had hurt so much;
with NATURE I walked to broken heart share;

I looked towards the mountains and saw the mountains;
I looked toward the sea and saw the ocean;
but when YOU I looked to find, YOU I couldn't see;
like I couldn't see the trees through my tears; lost you
    were to me;

I looked towards NATURE to settle my fears
and looked to the wind to dry my tears;
as I walked the wind also blew away the leaves;
to help me find the way through the trees;

NATURE'S wind and cold mist felt good;
and they tamed my heart's fears;
when I found my way home, my cheeks were dry
and there were no more tears;

Though the pain in my heart was still there,
I was no longer lost; my tears gone and my vision clear;
No longer was I lost; and my vision clear. . . .